WEEKLY **WR** READER®
EARLY LEARNING LIBRARY

Where People **Work**

¿Dónde **trabaja** la gente?

What Happens at a

Recycling Center?

¿Qué pasa en

un centro de reciclaje?

by/por Kathleen Pohl

Reading consultant/Consultora de lectura: Susan Nations, M.Ed., author, literacy coach, consultant in literacy development/autora, tutora de alfabetización, consultora de desarrollo de la lectura

Please visit our web site at: www.garethstevens.com
For a free color catalog describing Weekly Reader® Early Learning Library's list
of high-quality books, call 1-877-445-5824 (USA) or 1-800-387-3178 (Canada).
Weekly Reader® Early Learning Library's fax: (414) 336-0164.

Library of Congress Cataloging-in-Publication Data

Pohl, Kathleen.
    What happens at a recycling center? = ¿Qué pasa en un centro de reciclaje? / Kathleen Pohl.
      p. cm. — (Where people work = ¿Dónde trabaja la gente?)
    Includes bibliographical references and index.
    ISBN-10: 0-8368-7389-0 — ISBN-13: 978-0-8368-7389-4 (lib. bdg.)
    ISBN-10: 0-8368-7396-3 — ISBN-13: 978-0-8368-7396-2 (softcover)
    1. Recycling (Waste, etc.)—Juvenile literature. 2. Recycling centers—Juvenile literature. I. Title.
  II. Title: Qué pasa en un centro de reciclaje? III. Series: Pohl, Kathleen. Where people work (Spanish & English).
  TD792.P6418   2007a
  363.72'82—dc22   2006016872

This edition first published in 2007 by
Weekly Reader® Early Learning Library
A Member of the WRC Media Family of Companies
330 West Olive Street, Suite 100
Milwaukee, WI 53212 USA

Buddy® is a registered trademark of Weekly Reader Corporation. Used under license.

Managing editor: Dorothy L. Gibbs
Art direction: Tammy West
Cover design and page layout: Scott M. Krall
Picture research: Diane Laska-Swanke and Kathleen Pohl
Photographer: Jack Long
Translation: Tatiana Acosta and Guillermo Gutiérrez

Acknowledgments: The publisher thanks Brittany, Brooke, and Dana Bebo and Mary Jo Ward
and Jim Molenda for modeling in this book. Special thanks to Mary Jo and John Ward, of
National Salvage, Ltd., for their expert consulting and the use of their company's facilities.

Printed in the United States of America

1 2 3 4 5 6 7 8 9 10 09 08 07 06

Hi, Kids!

I'm Buddy, your Weekly Reader® pal. Have you ever visited a recycling center? I'm here to show and tell what happens at a recycling center. So, come on. Turn the page and read along!

– – – – – – – – –

¡Hola, chicos!

Soy Buddy, su amigo de Weekly Reader®. ¿Han estado alguna vez en un centro de reciclaje? Estoy aquí para contarles lo que pasa en un centro de reciclaje. Así que vengan conmigo. ¡Pasen la página y vamos a leer!

Do you know what this sign means? That's right. It means **recycle**! It tells us we should not throw away things we can use again. When we recycle, we help save Earth.

— — — — — — — — —

¿Saben lo que significa este signo? Muy bien. ¡Significa que hay que **reciclar**! Nos dice que no debemos tirar las cosas que podemos volver a usar. Cuando reciclamos, contribuimos a salvar la Tierra.

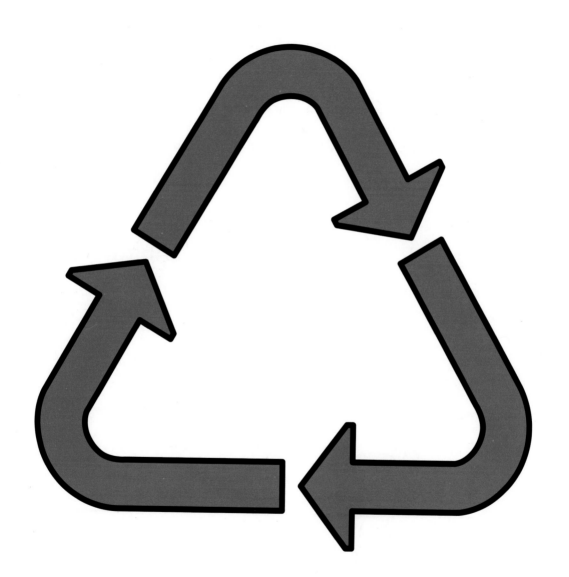

Brittany and Brooke are at a recycling center. They have some empty metal cans. Most of the cans are **aluminum**.

Brittany y Brooke están en un centro de reciclaje. Tienen algunas latas vacías. La mayoría de las latas son de **aluminio**.

Mrs. Ward works at the recycling center. She uses a **magnet** to find cans that are not aluminum. **Steel** cans stick to the magnet. Aluminum cans do not.

— — — — — — — —

La señora Ward trabaja en el centro de reciclaje. Usa un **imán** para encontrar las latas que no son de aluminio. El **acero** se pega al imán. Las latas de aluminio no se pegan.

magnet/imán

Mrs. Ward weighs the cans on a big **scale**. Now she knows how much to pay Brittany and Brooke for them.

— — — — — — — — —

La señora Ward pesa las latas en una gran **báscula**. Ahora ya sabe cuánto tiene que pagar a Brittany y Brooke por las latas.

control for scale/
control de
la báscula

scale/báscula

Jim is Mrs. Ward's helper. He runs a big machine. Jim dumps Brittany and Brooke's cans into a bin called a **hopper**.

– – – – – – – –

Jim es el ayudante de la señora Ward. Maneja una gran máquina. Jim echa las latas de Brittany y Brooke en un gran recipiente llamado **tolva**.

hopper/tolva

A **conveyor belt** carries the cans from the hopper to a can crusher. The crusher smashes the cans flat.

— — — — — — — —

Una **cinta transportadora** lleva las latas desde la tolva hasta una trituradora de latas. La trituradora aplasta las latas.

conveyor belt/cinta transportadora

can crusher/ trituradora de latas

hopper/tolva

15

The crusher also presses the cans into small squares. They are called **biscuits**. Hundreds of cans are in each biscuit.

— — — — — — — —

La trituradora también forma pequeños cubos con las latas. Estos cubos reciben el nombre de **balas**. En cada bala hay cientos de latas.

biscuit/bala

Jim makes big stacks of biscuits.
The stacks are called **bricks**. Stacks of
crushed cans are used to make new cans!

– – – – – – – – –

Jim hace grandes pilas de balas. Estas
pilas se llaman **briquetas**. ¡Las pilas de
latas aplastadas se usan para hacer
nuevas latas!

You can recycle cans, too! Do you have a recycling center near you?

— — — — — — — — —

¡Tú también puedes reciclar latas! ¿Hay un centro de reciclaje cerca de tu casa?

Recycling a Can/ Reciclaje de una lata

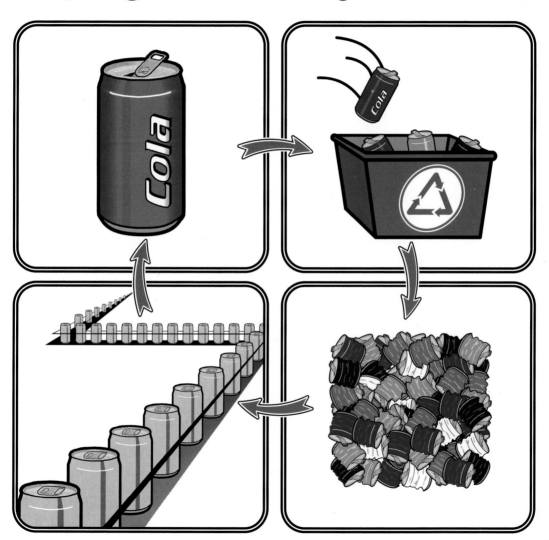

Glossary/Glosario

aluminum — a soft, lightweight metal that is used to make drink cans and many other products

conveyor belt — part of a machine that looks like a wide, flat belt and is used to move objects along in a line

magnet — a piece of metal with a special power to make iron or steel move toward it and stick to it

recyle — to use old materials to make new materials

steel — a hard, strong metal made of iron

— — — — — — — — —

acero — metal duro y fuerte que se hace con hierro

aluminio — metal ligero y blando que se usa para hacer latas de bebidas y muchos otros productos

cinta transportadora — parte de una máquina con forma de cinta, ancha y plana, que se usa para desplazar objetos

imán — pieza de metal que tiene la capacidad de atraer el hierro y el acero

reciclar — usar materiales viejos para hacer nuevos productos

For More Information/Más información

Books/Libros

Earth Day — Hooray!. Stuart J. Murphy (HarperCollins)

Follow that Trash: All About Recycling. Francine Jacobs
  (Grosset & Dunlap)

Recycle! A Handbook for Kids. Gail Gibbons (Little, Brown)

Recycling a Can. Cynthia MacGregor (Rosen)

Spyglass Books: Waste Not. Rebecca Weber
  (Compass Point Books)

# Index/Índice

About the Author

Kathleen Pohl has written and edited many children's books. Among them are animal tales, rhyming books, retold classics, and the forty-book series *Nature Close-Ups*. She also served for many years as top editor of *Taste of Home* and *Country Woman* magazines. She and her husband, Bruce, live among beautiful Wisconsin woods and share their home with six goats, a llama, and all kinds of wonderful woodland creatures.

Información sobre la autora

Kathleen Pohl ha escrito y corregido muchos libros infantiles. Entre ellos hay cuentos de animales, libros de rimas, versiones nuevas de cuentos clásicos y la serie de cuarenta libros *Nature Close-Ups*. Además, trabajó durante muchos años como directora de las revistas *Taste of Home* y *Country Woman*. Kathleen vive con su marido, Bruce, en los bellos bosques de Wisconsin. Ambos comparten su hogar con seis cabras, una llama y todo tipo de maravillosos animales del bosque.